HOMESTEAD BUDGETING

Knowing What It Costs, What It Returns, and When It Pays for Itself

Hudson Briggs

The Homestead Starter Series — Book 8

Disclaimer

This book provides general educational information. Building codes, soil conditions, animal regulations, weather, material availability, and prices vary by location. Confirm local rules and use appropriate safety practices before beginning any project.

A Note Before You Begin

This is Book 8, the last in The Homestead Starter Series, and it is the one that tells you the truth about money.

Homesteading is sold to beginners on a promise of savings. Grow your own food, keep your own hens, and watch the grocery bill fall. Some of that is true. A good deal of it is true eventually. Almost none of it is true in the first year, and nobody says so, which is why so many people conclude they must be doing it wrong when their first season costs more than it returns.

This book fixes that by doing arithmetic instead of making promises. It uses the actual verified figures from the rest of this series. When Chapter 7 works out what your eggs cost, it uses the coop and run prices from Book 6 and the feed consumption from Book 3, and it arrives at a number that is not flattering and is not meant to be: about eight dollars and sixty-seven cents a dozen in the first year, falling to about two dollars and seventy-five cents averaged across ten. Both numbers are real, and the difference between them is the entire subject of this book.

You will learn to keep simple records, to separate one-time costs from annual ones, to value what you produce without fooling yourself, to calculate when a project pays for itself, and to plan five years ahead rather than one season at a time.

The usual disclaimer, said once: prices vary by region and change over time, so every figure here is an example to be replaced with your own. Nothing in this book is tax, legal, or financial advice, and rules on selling what you produce vary considerably by jurisdiction.

Let's look at the numbers honestly.

Introduction

What You'll Learn

This introduction sets out what homestead budgeting actually involves, why it differs from ordinary household budgeting, and how the rest of the book builds from simple record keeping to a full five-year plan.

Why Money Is the Missing Chapter

Most homesteading guides cover growing, keeping, and building, and then go quiet about cost. The result is that beginners plan projects they cannot finish, expect savings that arrive years later than promised, and have no way to tell a genuinely good investment from a bad one.

Money is not the reason to homestead. But it is the reason most people stop, because they run out of it, or because the gap between the promised savings and the actual bank balance becomes discouraging. Understanding the numbers is what lets you keep going long enough to reach the point where the savings are real.

Why It Matters

Consider the pattern this series has already established. A raised bed costs about a hundred and ninety-one dollars to build and returns perhaps a hundred and eighty dollars of vegetables a year. A coop and run cost about seven hundred and ninety-three dollars and produce a hundred and twenty-five dozen eggs a year. A rabbit trio costs about four hundred and eighty-eight dollars and produces around a hundred and nineteen pounds of meat.

None of those pays for itself in the first season. All of them pay for themselves eventually, and the timeline is knowable in advance rather than a matter of faith.

Knowing which projects pay back in two years and which take five changes what you build first, and that single insight is worth more than any individual money-saving tip.

How This Book Works

The first two chapters cover the foundations: why homestead money behaves differently from household money, and how to keep records that take five minutes a week rather than an evening. Chapters 3 and 4 separate the two kinds of cost, the one-time and the ongoing, which is the distinction that makes everything else possible. Chapter 5 tackles the hardest and most self-deceiving part, valuing what you produce. Chapter 6 gives you the break-even calculation.

Then come three chapters of full worked examples, using real numbers from across this series: eggs, meat and milk, and the garden. Chapter 10 answers the build-or-buy question. Chapter 11 covers reducing costs and selling surplus. The final chapter assembles a five-year budget.

Action Plan

Before the next chapter, find last month's grocery receipts, or your banking app, and work out roughly what you spend on food in a month. That single number is the baseline every calculation in this book measures against, and most people have never actually looked at it.

Chapter 1: Why Homestead Budgeting Is Different

What You'll Learn

This chapter explains the four ways homestead money behaves differently from household money: the split between capital and operating costs, the seasonality of both spending and returns, the portion of the return that never appears as cash, and the question of whether to count your own labour.

Why It Matters

Applying ordinary household budgeting to a homestead produces conclusions that are wrong in both directions. It makes year one look like a disaster, because you are comparing a year of setup spending against a year of partial production. And it can make year five look better than it is, if you have quietly forgotten the capital you sank at the start. Getting the framework right is what makes the numbers mean something.

Capital Versus Operating

This is the central distinction in the entire book, and nearly every confused homestead calculation comes from mixing the two.

A capital cost is one-time. The coop, the raised bed, the fencing, the breeding stock, the incubator. You pay once and it serves for years. An operating cost is recurring. Feed, bedding, seeds, soil amendments, replacement stock, veterinary care.

The mistake beginners make is dividing a single year's total spending by a single year's production. That charges the entire coop against the first year of eggs and produces an alarming figure that says nothing useful about whether keeping hens is worthwhile. The coop will still be standing in ten years. Its cost belongs spread across those years, not dumped on the first one.

Which Kind of Cost Is Which

Capital, paid once	Operating, paid every year
Coop, run, and fencing	Feed
Raised beds and soil to fill them	Seeds and transplants
Hutches, cages, and nest boxes	Bedding and straw
Breeding stock and starter flock	Soil amendments and compost inputs
Tools, canner, incubator	Replacement stock and veterinary costs
Compost bins and water systems	Utilities, mineral supplements, and consumables

The practical rule: if it will still be there in three years, it is capital. If you will buy it again next spring, it is operating.

Everything Is Seasonal

Homestead spending and homestead returns arrive at opposite ends of the year, which strains a budget in a way ordinary household spending does not.

You buy seeds, chicks, soil, and lumber in late winter and spring, which is when spending peaks and returns are zero. Production arrives in summer and autumn. Winter brings continued feed costs with reduced output, since hens lay less in short days and nothing grows outside.

This means a homestead needs its spending anticipated and set aside months ahead. A budget built on monthly averages will be badly wrong in both March and September. Chapter 12 handles this with a seasonal plan rather than a monthly one.

The Return That Is Not Cash

A significant portion of what a homestead returns never shows up as money, and any honest accounting has to acknowledge it without using it as an excuse.

Some of it is measurable in principle: the quality of an egg from a hen you know, the absence of anything you did not choose to put on your food, produce picked an hour before it is eaten. Some of it is resilience, meaning food that does not depend on a supply chain or a paycheque. Some of it is skill, which compounds, and some of it is simply that many people find the work deeply satisfying.

None of that pays for lumber. The honest position is to calculate the cash figures rigorously, then decide separately whether the non-cash return justifies whatever gap remains. What you should not do is use the non-cash return to avoid doing the arithmetic, which is the most common form of homestead self-deception.

Should You Count Your Labour?

This question causes more arguments than any other in homestead economics, and the answer depends on what you are trying to decide.

If you are deciding whether a project is a good use of your time compared with paid work, then yes, count it, and most homestead activities will lose that comparison badly. Growing your own vegetables rarely beats an hourly wage.

If you are deciding between two homestead projects, count labour, because time is your scarcest resource and the comparison is fair.

If you are deciding whether homesteading is worth doing at all, counting labour misses the point, because for most people the work is part of the reward rather than a cost paid to obtain it. Nobody costs their own gardening hours against a wage and concludes they should watch television instead.

This book takes the middle position throughout: cash costs are counted precisely, and labour is tracked in hours rather than converted to dollars, so you can see where your time goes without pretending an afternoon in the garden is a business expense.

Common Mistakes

Charging a one-time capital cost entirely against the first year's production.

Budgeting monthly averages for spending that is overwhelmingly seasonal.

Using non-cash benefits to avoid doing the cash arithmetic at all.

Comparing homestead output against premium organic retail prices to make the numbers look good.

Forgetting capital entirely by year three, and concluding the eggs are nearly free.

Costing your own labour at a wage and concluding the whole enterprise is irrational.

Budget Options

The free or near-free path: The framework in this chapter costs nothing and is the most valuable budgeting tool in the book. Separating capital from operating in a notebook, and setting aside money in winter for spring spending, prevents most homestead financial trouble without any system at all.

The starter path: A simple spreadsheet with two sheets, one for capital purchases with dates and expected life, one for annual operating costs by category, gives you everything the rest of this book needs and takes an hour to set up.

Quick Wins

Sort every homestead expense into capital or operating, starting today.

Apply the three-year rule when you are unsure which it is.

Set money aside in autumn for the spring spending peak.

Track your hours, but do not convert them to dollars.

Compare your output against what you would actually have bought, not the premium version.

Chapter Checklist

- [ ] I understand the difference between capital and operating costs
- [ ] I know which of my existing homestead expenses are which
- [ ] I have anticipated the spring spending peak
- [ ] I have decided how to treat non-cash returns honestly
- [ ] I have decided how to treat my own labour, and why
- [ ] I will compare output against realistic prices, not premium ones

Action Plan

List every homestead expense you can remember from the past year and sort it into two columns, capital and operating, applying the three-year rule to anything uncertain. Note roughly when in the year each was spent. That single page is the raw material for everything that follows, and the next chapter turns it into a record system you will actually maintain.

Chapter 2: Records That Take Five Minutes a Week

What You'll Learn

This chapter sets up a record system simple enough that you will still be using it in October. You will learn the four things worth tracking, the three things that are not worth tracking, how to capture receipts without effort, and how to review the numbers once a season.

Why It Matters

Every calculation in the rest of this book depends on knowing what you actually spent and produced. Nearly every beginner starts an elaborate tracking system in February and abandons it by May, which leaves them with two months of excellent data and no idea what the year cost.

The system that works is the one small enough to survive the busy season. Five minutes a week, done all year, beats a detailed system done for six weeks.

Track Four Things

Money out, split into capital and operating. Date, amount, category, and which enterprise it belongs to, meaning the garden, the flock, the rabbits. Four words and a number.

What you produced. Eggs collected, pounds harvested, pounds of meat, quarts of milk. A tally sheet on the coop door is entirely sufficient for eggs, and a kitchen scale and a notebook cover the garden.

Money in, if any. Surplus eggs sold, extra seedlings, stock sold to other keepers.

Hours, roughly. Not to the minute, and not converted to money. Just enough to know whether an enterprise is consuming your Saturdays.

A Record System You Will Actually Keep

What	How Often	Where	Time Needed
Money out, capital	When it happens	Phone photo of receipt	Seconds
Money out, operating	When it happens	Phone photo of receipt	Seconds
Eggs collected	Daily	Tally sheet on the coop door	Seconds
Harvest weight	At harvest	Kitchen scale and notebook	A minute
Meat and milk	At processing or milking	Notebook	A minute
Money in	When it happens	Same notebook	Seconds
Hours	Weekly estimate	Notebook	A minute
Review and total	Seasonally	Spreadsheet or notebook	Half an hour

Do Not Track These

Every individual vegetable. Weighing each radish produces data nobody uses. Weigh by crop and by harvest, or simply weigh the basket.

Utilities to three decimal places. Unless you have a specific large draw such as a heated waterer or a well pump, the difference is lost in the noise.

Your own labour in dollars. As Chapter 1 explains, track hours, not wages.

The instinct to track everything is what kills record systems. Track what changes a decision.

The Receipt Problem

The main practical failure is receipts, which accumulate in pockets and vanish. The solution is a phone photo at the point of purchase, into a folder or album named for the year. It takes two seconds and it means the record exists even if you never file the paper.

Once a season, sit down with the photos and enter them. Twenty minutes four times a year is a complete financial record.

Simple Enterprise Accounting

The most useful refinement is separating your homestead into enterprises and tracking each on its own. The garden, the flock, the rabbits, the orchard. This is the difference between knowing that your homestead cost eleven hundred dollars and knowing that the garden nearly pays for itself while the goats are consuming everything.

Give each enterprise a page or a column. Assign every cost to one. Shared costs, such as a fence that serves two purposes, can simply be split roughly, since precision is not the point.

The Seasonal Review

Four times a year, at the turn of each season, spend half an hour on three questions.

What did this enterprise cost this season, and what did it produce? Is the trend going the direction I expected? And is there one change that would improve it materially next season?

That last question is the whole reason for keeping records. Data that never changes a decision is a hobby, and the point of this system is to tell you that your feed cost jumped when you switched suppliers, or that the second raised bed produced almost as much as the first for a fifth of the setup cost.

Common Mistakes

Building an elaborate system in winter that collapses in June.

Tracking every individual item instead of the categories that inform decisions.

Losing receipts, which are the only record of capital spending.

Lumping all enterprises together, so a profitable garden hides an expensive flock.

Recording costs but never recording production, which makes every ratio impossible.

Reviewing only at year end, too late to change anything.

Budget Options

The free or near-free path: A notebook, a tally sheet on the coop door, and a phone camera for receipts. This costs nothing and is entirely sufficient for a small homestead, and it is what most successful small keepers actually use.

The starter path: A spreadsheet with a sheet per enterprise, entered seasonally from receipt photos, giving you sortable multi-year data that makes the five-year planning in Chapter 12 straightforward.

Quick Wins

Photograph every receipt at the till, into a folder named for the year.

Put a tally sheet and a pencil on the coop door today.

Give each enterprise its own page or column.

Weigh harvests by the basket, not by the vegetable.

Book half an hour at the turn of each season to review.

Chapter Checklist

[ ] I am recording money out, split capital and operating, by enterprise

[ ] I am recording production: eggs, weights, quarts

[ ] I am recording any money in

[ ] I am roughly tracking hours, without converting them to dollars

[ ] I photograph receipts at the point of purchase

[ ] Each enterprise is tracked separately

[ ] I have a seasonal review scheduled

Action Plan

Set up the system this week while it is quiet. Create a photo album for receipts, put a tally sheet on the coop door, and start a page for each enterprise you run. Then enter whatever you already have from this year, however incomplete. With records running, the next chapter looks at the first half of the picture: what it actually costs to start.

Chapter 3: Startup Costs - What It Really Takes to Begin

What You'll Learn

This chapter puts real numbers on starting each part of a homestead, using the verified build costs from Book 6 and the stock and equipment costs from Book 7. You will see what a minimum start costs, what a full setup costs, and how to phase the spending so it does not all land in one spring.

Why It Matters

Startup cost is where homesteading dreams meet a bank balance, and vague estimates are what cause half-finished projects. A person who believes a chicken setup costs two hundred dollars and discovers it costs eight hundred often stops partway, ending up with a coop and no run, which is worse than either finishing or not starting.

Knowing the real figure in advance lets you either save for it, phase it, or choose a cheaper enterprise deliberately.

What Each Enterprise Costs to Start

Every figure below comes from the verified build costs in Book 6 and the equipment and stock costs in Book 7, at the example prices those books use.

What It Costs to Begin Each Part of a Homestead

Enterprise	What It Includes	Startup Cost
One raised bed	Bed, soil, and screws	191 dollars
Full garden setup	Bed, cold frame, compost bins, bench, trellis, fence	780 dollars
Flock of six hens	Coop, run, feeder stand, and six chicks	823 dollars
Quail, six birds	Cage, feeders, feed, and birds	185 dollars
Ducks, six birds	Shelter, feeders, feed, and ducklings	233 dollars
Rabbit breeding trio	Hutches, equipment, feed, and stock	488 dollars
Two dairy goats	Fencing, shelter, stand, minerals, and does	1525 dollars

Two observations worth drawing out. First, the coop and run dominate the chicken figure, at seven hundred and ninety-three dollars of the eight hundred and twenty-three, while the birds themselves cost thirty. The housing is the project; the animals are almost an afterthought financially. Second, goats cost roughly three times a rabbit setup and nearly twice a full garden, which is the financial version of the warning Book 7 gives about goats being the largest commitment in the series.

The Cheapest Real Start

If money is the binding constraint, the cheapest genuine entries are quail at about a hundred and eighty-five dollars and a single raised bed at about a hundred and ninety-one. Both are complete, functioning enterprises rather than partial setups, and both produce food in their first season.

That matters more than it appears. A finished small project beats a half-finished large one in every respect: it produces, it teaches, and it does not sit in the yard as a reproach. Chapter 12 builds on this principle directly.

Where the Money Actually Goes

Across nearly every enterprise, the pattern is the same: housing and infrastructure dominate, and the living things are cheap.

Six chicks cost thirty dollars and their housing costs seven hundred and ninety-three. A rabbit trio costs a hundred and twenty dollars and the cages, equipment, and first feed cost three hundred and sixty-eight. Goat fencing and shelter cost more than a beginner expects and roughly match the price of the animals.

This is why building rather than buying, covered fully in Chapter 10, is the single largest lever on homestead startup cost. It is also why the cheapest way to expand is almost always to add animals to infrastructure you already own rather than to start a new enterprise.

Phasing the Spending

Nobody needs to buy all of this at once, and the sequence that works spreads capital across seasons rather than concentrating it.

Build in the off season when you have time and lumber prices are typically softer. Buy livestock in spring when chicks, ducklings, and kits are widely available and cheap. Add the second bed the following year out of the savings the first one generated. Buy the cold frame materials in late summer for the following spring rather than in the panic of March.

A homestead built across three years costs the same as one built in one spring and is far more likely to be finished, because each stage is paid for and functioning before the next begins.

Spreading Startup Across Three Years

Year	What You Add	Approximate Capital
Year 1	One raised bed and a compost system	385 dollars
Year 2	Coop, run, and a flock of six hens	823 dollars
Year 3	Rabbit trio and remaining garden projects	883 dollars
Three-year total	A working garden, flock, and meat supply	2091 dollars

Reducing Startup Without Compromising

Some savings are free and some are false economies, and the distinction matters more at startup than anywhere else.

Genuine savings: building rather than buying, using reclaimed lumber, buying stock locally rather than shipped, starting from chicks or kits rather than adult animals, borrowing tools for a single build, and buying materials off season.

False economies: chicken wire instead of hardware cloth, undersized housing you will replace within two years, cheap fencing for goats, and buying poor-quality breeding stock. Every one of those costs more within three years than the saving was worth, and Books 3, 6, and 7 explain why in detail.

Common Mistakes

Underestimating housing, which is the dominant cost in every animal enterprise.

Starting a large project without the capital to finish it, and leaving it half done.

Buying all infrastructure in one spring, straining the budget at the worst point in the year.

Economising on hardware cloth, fencing, or breeding stock, which costs more within a few years.

Buying adult animals when chicks or kits would do.

Assuming the animals are the expensive part; they almost never are.

Budget Options

The free or near-free path: Build every structure from reclaimed material using the plans in Book 6, which is the largest single reduction available, and start with quail or one raised bed. A functioning homestead enterprise can be started for well under two hundred dollars this way.

The starter path: Build your own structures from new material and buy quality stock, which is the approach costed throughout this series and which produces infrastructure that lasts a decade or more without replacement.

Quick Wins

Price your housing before you price your animals; that is where the money is.

Finish one small enterprise rather than starting a large one you cannot complete.

Build in the off season and buy livestock in spring.

Never economise on hardware cloth, latches, or goat fencing.

Add animals to existing infrastructure before starting a new enterprise.

Chapter Checklist

[ ] I know the real startup cost of the enterprise I want

[ ] I have the capital to finish it, not just to begin it

[ ] I have considered building rather than buying the infrastructure

[ ] I have phased my spending across seasons rather than one spring

[ ] I have not economised on the items that must be bought properly

[ ] I am starting with something I can complete

Action Plan

Pick the enterprise you want and write down its startup figure from the table in this chapter. Check that number against what you can actually spend this year, and if the gap is large, either choose a smaller enterprise or phase it across two seasons. Then price the same project with reclaimed materials and Book 6 plans to see the real range. The next chapter covers the costs that arrive every year thereafter.

Chapter 4: Operating Costs - The Annual Reality

What You'll Learn

This chapter covers what a homestead costs every year once it is built: feed, bedding, seeds, amendments, replacement stock, and the small recurring items that add up. You will see real annual figures for a garden, a flock, and a rabbitry, drawn from the feed consumption established in Books 3 and 7.

Why It Matters

Capital costs are visible and frightening, so people plan for them. Operating costs are small, frequent, and invisible, so people do not, and that is where budgets actually fail. A bag of feed here and a bale of straw there does not feel like a financial decision, but across a year it is the larger number for most enterprises after the second season.

What Each Enterprise Costs Per Year

What It Costs to Run Each Year

Enterprise	Main Costs	Annual Cost
One raised bed	Seeds, transplants, amendments	50 dollars
Full garden setup	Seeds, transplants, amendments, compost inputs	150 dollars
Flock of six hens	Feed 206, bedding 40, grit and shell 15	261 dollars
Rabbit breeding trio	Pellets 521, hay 80, bedding 40	641 dollars

The flock figure comes directly from Book 3, where six hens eating one and a half pounds a week each consume four hundred and sixty-eight pounds a year, costing about two hundred and six dollars at twenty-two dollars per fifty-pound bag. The rabbit figure comes from Book 7, where a trio and their offspring consume about one thousand and forty-two pounds of pellets a year at fifty cents a pound.

Notice that the rabbitry costs more to run annually than the flock, despite costing less to set up. That reversal is common and is exactly why both numbers matter.

Feed Is the Dominant Cost

For any animal enterprise, feed is the largest recurring expense by a wide margin, typically seventy to eighty percent of annual operating cost. Everything else is rounding by comparison.

This means feed is where cost reduction efforts should concentrate, and Chapter 11 covers that in detail. It also means that the price you pay per bag has an outsized effect on your final cost per egg or per pound. Book 3 makes this explicit by showing feed cost at both twenty-two and thirty dollars per bag, a difference that moves the annual cost for six hens from two hundred and six dollars to two hundred and eighty-one.

Track your actual feed price. It is the single most consequential number in your operating budget.

The Costs People Forget

Several recurring costs are genuinely easy to overlook and reliably appear anyway.

Replacement stock. Hens lay strongly for two to three years, as Book 3 explains, but live far longer. Sustaining production means adding new birds periodically, whether by buying chicks or hatching your own. Budget for it rather than being surprised by it.

Bedding. Straw or shavings are cheap per bale and constant across a year.

Health and consumables. Grit, oyster shell, minerals, dewormer, and the occasional veterinary call. Small most years and occasionally not.

Water and utilities. Usually negligible, unless you run heated waterers through a long winter or pump irrigation water, in which case it is worth measuring rather than guessing.

Soil. A raised bed settles and needs topping up with compost annually, which is either a cash cost or an argument for the compost system in Book 5.

Reducing Operating Costs Legitimately

Two levers do most of the work, and both are covered fully in Chapter 11.

Buying feed in bulk reduces the per-pound price meaningfully, limited only by dry storage and by how quickly you use it before it goes stale. And producing inputs yourself, particularly compost from Book 5 instead of bought amendments, converts a cash cost into a use for waste you already have.

Forage and garden surplus reduce feed bills for poultry and rabbits, though not as dramatically as beginners hope. Geese are the exception, as Book 7 notes, since they genuinely graze most of their summer diet.

Common Mistakes

Planning capital carefully and operating costs not at all.

Not knowing your actual feed price per pound, which drives most of the total.

Forgetting replacement stock, then facing a sudden drop in production.

Assuming foraging will replace most of the feed bill; it will not, except for geese.

Buying feed in small bags at a premium because storage was never set up.

Overlooking annual soil top-up in raised beds.

Budget Options

The free or near-free path: Compost from Book 5 replaces bought soil amendments entirely, kitchen and garden surplus supplements feed, and saved seed reduces the garden's annual cost to almost nothing beyond transplants.

The starter path: Buy feed in the largest bags your storage allows, keep a running note of the per-pound price, and budget a fixed amount annually for replacement stock so it never arrives as a surprise.

Quick Wins

Work out your feed price per pound today, and write it down.

Buy the largest feed bag you can store dry and use before it stales.

Budget replacement stock every year, not every third year in a panic.

Use compost from Book 5 rather than buying amendments.

Top up raised bed soil annually and count it as an operating cost.

Chapter Checklist

[ ] I know my annual operating cost for each enterprise

[ ] I know my feed price per pound

[ ] I have budgeted for replacement stock

[ ] I have accounted for bedding, grit, minerals, and consumables

[ ] I have accounted for annual soil top-up in raised beds

[ ] I have identified my two biggest reduction opportunities

Action Plan

Total your operating costs for each enterprise over the past year from the records you set up in Chapter 2, or estimate them from the table here if you have no records yet. Work out your feed price per pound and write it somewhere you will see it. Identify the two largest lines and mark them for the reduction strategies in Chapter 11. With both halves of the cost picture in place, the next chapter tackles the other side of the ledger: what your production is actually worth.

Chapter 5: Valuing What You Produce

What You'll Learn

This chapter covers the hardest and most self-deceiving part of homestead accounting: deciding what your own production is worth. You will learn the substitution rule that keeps valuations honest, why comparing against premium retail prices ruins the calculation, how to handle surplus you would never have bought, and what quality is legitimately worth.

Why It Matters

Every break-even calculation, every build-or-buy decision, and every judgement about whether an enterprise is worth continuing depends on the value you assign to what you produce. Inflate it and you will conclude that a costly enterprise is thriving. Undervalue it and you will abandon something that was working.

This is also where most published homestead economics goes wrong, almost always in the flattering direction.

The Substitution Rule

The governing principle is simple: value your production at what you would otherwise actually have bought.

Not what it might sell for. Not the premium version. What would genuinely have been in your trolley if you did not produce it.

If you buy standard supermarket eggs at four dollars a dozen, your eggs are worth four dollars a dozen, even though pastured eggs from a farm stand sell for nine. If you would never have paid nine dollars, then producing a nine dollar egg has not saved you nine dollars; it has saved you four.

This single rule eliminates most homestead accounting fantasy. It is also why this book values eggs at four dollars a dozen throughout, rabbit at seven dollars a pound, and vegetables at three dollars a pound, all ordinary prices rather than boutique ones.

The Substitution Rule Applied

Product	Premium Retail	What This Book Uses	Why
Eggs, per dozen	8 to 9 dollars	4 dollars	What most people actually buy
Rabbit meat, per pound	12 dollars or more	7 dollars	Comparable to good butcher meat
Vegetables, per pound	5 dollars organic	3 dollars	Ordinary supermarket produce
Goat milk, per gallon	14 dollars or more	8 dollars	Well above cow milk, below boutique

The Sixty-Four Dollar Tomato

There is a well-known trap in which a gardener spends heavily on beds, soil, tools, irrigation, and amendments, harvests a modest crop in the first season, divides one by the other, and discovers each tomato cost an absurd amount.

The arithmetic is correct and the conclusion is wrong, for the reason Chapter 1 established: it charges the entire capital cost against a single season. The bed will produce for a decade. Spread properly, the tomato is ordinary.

But the trap contains a real warning. If you keep buying new capital every season, a new bed, a new tool, a new system, you never reach the years in which the earlier capital pays off. The gardener who builds one bed and uses it for ten years does well. The gardener who builds a new bed every spring is permanently in year one, and their tomatoes really do cost sixty-four dollars.

Do Not Count What You Would Not Have Bought

The second great inflation is counting surplus at full value.

If your garden produces forty pounds of zucchini and you would have bought four, you have saved the price of four pounds. The other thirty-six are genuinely worth something, since they can be preserved with Book 4, fed to livestock, given away, or composted, but they are not worth three dollars a pound of grocery savings.

The honest treatment is to value at substitution price up to the quantity you would have bought, and to value the surplus at whatever it actually displaces, which is often feed cost or nothing.

The same applies to eggs. Six hens producing a hundred and twenty-five dozen a year is far more than most households eat. If you use eighty dozen and give away forty-five, your saving is eighty dozen, unless you sell the rest, which Chapter 11 covers.

This is one of the strongest practical arguments for matching your production to your consumption rather than maximising it.

What Quality Is Legitimately Worth

None of this means quality counts for nothing. It means quality should be valued deliberately rather than assumed.

If you genuinely would have bought pastured eggs at eight dollars because you care about how the hens live, then eight dollars is your substitution price and your eggs are worth it. The test is whether you were actually buying the premium product before, or whether you are retrospectively upgrading your baseline to make the numbers work.

Be honest about which. Both answers are respectable; only one of them is true for you.

Beyond substitution, there are returns that do not convert to money at all, as Chapter 1 discussed: control over inputs, freshness, resilience, and the satisfaction of the work. Keep those out of the arithmetic and weigh them separately when you decide whether a gap is acceptable.

A Worked Valuation

Here is a full year of production for the combined homestead this book uses as its example, valued by the substitution rule.

What a Garden, Flock, and Rabbitry Produce in a Year

Enterprise	Annual Production	Substitution Price	Value
One raised bed	60 pounds of vegetables	3 dollars per pound	180 dollars
Six hens	125 dozen eggs	4 dollars per dozen	500 dollars
Rabbit trio	119 pounds dressed meat	7 dollars per pound	833 dollars
Combined annual value	all three enterprises	at substitution prices	1513 dollars

Fifteen hundred dollars of food a year from a garden bed, six hens, and three rabbits is a genuinely meaningful contribution to a household. What it costs to obtain is the subject of the next chapter.

Common Mistakes

Valuing production at premium retail prices you would never actually pay.

Charging all capital against the first season and concluding the produce is absurdly expensive.

Counting every pound of surplus at full grocery value.

Retrospectively upgrading your baseline to make an enterprise look better.

Producing far more than you consume and counting the excess as savings.

Building new capital every season, so earlier capital never pays off.

Budget Options

The free or near-free path: Match production to consumption rather than maximising it, which costs nothing and immediately improves your real return. Preserve surplus with Book 4 so it displaces future purchases rather than being wasted.

The starter path: Record what you actually buy for a month, use those exact prices as your substitution values, and you will have the most accurate valuation possible for your own household.

Quick Wins

Use the price you actually pay, not the premium version.

Value surplus at what it displaces, not at grocery prices.

Spread capital across the years it will serve.

Match production to what your household eats.

Keep non-cash benefits out of the arithmetic and weigh them separately.

Chapter Checklist

[ ] I am valuing production at what I would actually have bought

[ ] I have not inflated my baseline to premium prices

[ ] I am counting surplus at what it displaces, not full retail

[ ] I am spreading capital across its useful life

[ ] I have a sense of how much of my production I actually consume

[ ] I am weighing non-cash returns separately, not folding them into the numbers

Action Plan

Write down the prices you actually pay for eggs, meat, and vegetables, from a recent receipt rather than memory. Those are your substitution values, and every calculation in the rest of this book should use them in place of the examples. Then estimate honestly how much of your production your household actually consumes. With costs and value both established, the next chapter combines them into the calculation that answers the real question.

Chapter 6: Break-Even - The Calculation That Matters

What You'll Learn

This chapter gives you the one calculation that answers whether a homestead project is worth doing: how long it takes to pay for itself. You will learn the formula, apply it to each enterprise in this series, see what changes the answer, and learn to recognise the projects that never break even and decide about them honestly.

Why It Matters

Every other number in this book is input to this one. Break-even is what tells you that a raised bed pays for itself in about a season and a half while a coop and run take over three years, and that difference should shape what you build first, particularly if money is tight.

It also protects you from the two opposite errors: abandoning a good project in year one because it has not paid off yet, and continuing a bad one for years because you never checked.

The Formula

Break-even in years equals capital cost divided by annual surplus, where annual surplus is the value of what you produce minus what it costs to operate.

That is the whole calculation. In practice:

First, take the capital cost, the one-time spending from Chapter 3. Second, take the annual value of production, using the substitution prices from Chapter 5. Third, subtract the annual operating cost from Chapter 4, which gives you the annual surplus. Fourth, divide the capital by that surplus.

If the annual surplus is zero or negative, the project never breaks even, which is important information rather than a failure of the method.

Applied to Each Enterprise

How Long Each Project Takes to Pay for Itself

Enterprise	Capital	Annual Value	Annual Operating	Annual Surplus	Break-Even
One raised bed	191 dollars	180 dollars	50 dollars	130 dollars	1.5 years
Rabbit trio	488 dollars	833 dollars	641 dollars	192 dollars	2.5 years
Flock of six hens	823 dollars	500 dollars	261 dollars	239 dollars	3.4 years
All three combined	1502 dollars	1513 dollars	952 dollars	561 dollars	2.7 years

Read that table carefully, because it contains the most useful single insight in this book: the cheapest project pays back fastest. A raised bed returns its cost in about a season and a half. The flock, which costs more than four times as much to set up, takes well over twice as long.

This is the arithmetic behind the advice that runs through the whole series, that beginners should start small and finish what they start. It is not merely gentler counsel; it is the financially correct order.

What Changes the Answer

Four things move break-even substantially, and it is worth knowing which lever to pull.

Reducing capital has the largest effect and is almost entirely within your control. Building rather than buying, covered in Chapter 10, can halve the capital of most projects, which halves the break-even period directly.

Reducing operating cost is the second lever, mostly feed, as Chapter 4 established. Cutting a rabbitry's feed bill by fifteen percent moves its break-even by several months.

Increasing production helps if it is production you actually consume. Adding hens to an existing coop is unusually effective, because it raises output with almost no additional capital.

Your substitution price matters more than people expect. A household that genuinely buys premium eggs sees the flock break even far faster than one that buys the cheapest available, and neither is wrong; they simply have different baselines.

When Break-Even Never Arrives

Some enterprises will not pay for themselves, and pretending otherwise helps nobody.

Two dairy goats at about fifteen hundred dollars of capital, with substantial annual feed and hay costs, producing milk for a household that drinks little of it, may never generate a positive annual surplus. The same is true of a large flock kept by a household that eats six eggs a week, or any enterprise producing far beyond what its household consumes.

That does not automatically mean you should not do it. It means you should know that you are buying an experience, a skill, or a way of living rather than making an investment, and that the honest framing is a hobby cost rather than a saving. Many worthwhile things are hobbies. The failure is not knowing which one you are doing.

Beyond Break-Even

Once a project passes break-even, its economics change completely, and this is the part beginners never see because they quit before reaching it.

After the capital is recovered, the annual surplus is pure return. The raised bed that took a season and a half to pay for itself then delivers a hundred and thirty dollars a year for the remaining life of the bed, which with cedar is many years. The flock delivers two hundred and thirty-nine dollars a year once the coop is paid off, and the coop from Book 6 is built to last a decade or more.

That is the actual promise of homesteading, and it arrives in years three through ten rather than in year one. Everything in this book is designed to get you there.

Common Mistakes

Judging a project by its first year, which is always the worst year.

Failing to run the calculation at all, and continuing an enterprise on faith.

Building expensive infrastructure first, which delays break-even the longest.

Ignoring an enterprise that will never break even rather than deciding about it deliberately.

Comparing against premium prices to force a favourable answer.

Quitting in year two, just before the returns begin.

Budget Options

The free or near-free path: Reducing capital is the most powerful lever available, and building from Book 6 plans with reclaimed material can cut break-even times roughly in half across every project in this book.

The starter path: Run the calculation before each new project, build the fastest-payback projects first, and reinvest the surplus from each into the next, which compounds the whole homestead without additional outside money.

Quick Wins

Run the formula on your next project before you buy anything.

Build the fastest-payback project first, which is usually the cheapest.

Add animals to existing infrastructure to raise output without capital.

Use your own substitution prices, not the examples.

Name your hobby enterprises honestly, and keep them if you want them.

Chapter Checklist

[ ] I can calculate break-even: capital divided by annual surplus

[ ] I know the break-even period for each of my enterprises

[ ] I am building the fastest-payback projects first

[ ] I have identified which lever most improves my worst project

[ ] I have identified any enterprise that will never break even

[ ] I have decided deliberately whether to keep those anyway

Action Plan

Run the calculation for every enterprise you have or plan to have, using your own capital, operating, and substitution figures rather than the examples. Rank them by break-even period and build in that order. For anything that never breaks even, decide deliberately whether it is worth keeping as a hobby, and be at peace with the answer. The next three chapters work through the calculation in full detail, one enterprise at a time, starting with eggs.

Chapter 7: Eggs - A Full Worked Example

What You'll Learn

This chapter works out, from beginning to end, what backyard eggs actually cost. You will see the capital, the annual operating cost, the production, the cost per dozen in year one and averaged over ten years, and the point at which the flock has paid for itself. Every figure comes from Book 3 and Book 6.

Why It Matters

Eggs are the most common homestead enterprise and the one most often claimed to save money. This chapter tests that claim properly, and the answer is genuinely interesting: keeping hens is expensive in year one and clearly worthwhile by year four, and almost nobody tells beginners that in advance.

The Setup

Six hens, housed in the four-by-six coop and six-by-ten run built in Book 6, with the feeder stand and dust bath from the same book. Six hens is the flock size Book 3 sizes its coop for, at four square feet per bird.

One-Time Costs for a Flock of Six

Item	Source	Cost
Coop, 4 by 6 feet	Book 6, Chapter 6	457 dollars
Run, 6 by 10 feet	Book 6, Chapter 7	294 dollars
Feeder stand and dust bath	Book 6, Chapter 8	42 dollars
Six chicks	at 5 dollars each	30 dollars
Total capital	one-time	823 dollars

The Annual Cost

Feed comes straight from Book 3: a laying hen eats about one and a half pounds a week, so six hens eat nine pounds a week, or four hundred and sixty-eight pounds a year. At twenty-two dollars per fifty-pound bag, which is forty-four cents a pound, that is about two hundred and six dollars.

What Six Hens Cost Every Year

Item	Basis	Annual Cost
Feed	468 pounds at 44 cents	206 dollars
Bedding	straw or shavings	40 dollars
Grit and oyster shell	consumables	15 dollars
Total operating	every year	261 dollars

The Production

Six hens of a good laying breed produce about two hundred and fifty eggs each a year, which is within the range Book 3 gives for Australorps, Leghorns, sex-links, and similar. That is fifteen hundred eggs, or a hundred and twenty-five dozen.

The Cost Per Dozen

This is the calculation everyone wants, and it has three honest answers depending on what you include.

Three Honest Answers

Basis	Calculation	Cost per Dozen
Feed only	206 dollars over 125 dozen	1 dollar 65 cents
All operating costs	261 dollars over 125 dozen	2 dollars 9 cents
Year one, including all capital	1084 dollars over 125 dozen	8 dollars 67 cents
Averaged over five years	2128 dollars over 625 dozen	3 dollars 40 cents
Averaged over ten years	3433 dollars over 1250 dozen	2 dollars 75 cents

Those five numbers are all correct and all describe the same flock. Which one is honest depends on the question. If you are asking what the next dozen costs you, it is one dollar sixty-five. If you are asking what you spent this year divided by what you got, in year one, it is eight dollars sixty-seven. If you are asking whether keeping hens is a sound decision over the life of a coop, the ten-year figure of two dollars seventy-five is the right one.

Homesteading marketing quotes the first number. Sceptical articles quote the third. The truthful answer for someone deciding whether to keep hens is the last.

When the Flock Pays for Itself

Valuing eggs at four dollars a dozen by the substitution rule from Chapter 5, a hundred and twenty-five dozen is worth five hundred dollars a year. Operating costs are two hundred and sixty-one, so the annual surplus is two hundred and thirty-nine dollars.

Capital of eight hundred and twenty-three dollars divided by a surplus of two hundred and thirty-nine gives a break-even of about three and a half years.

From year four onward, the flock returns roughly two hundred and thirty-nine dollars a year of value against costs already paid, for as long as the coop stands, which for a coop built to the Book 6 specification is a decade or more.

What Changes This

Building the coop cheaply. Reclaimed materials can cut the capital by half or more, which cuts break-even to under two years. This is by far the largest lever.

Your feed price. Book 3 shows the same flock costing two hundred and eighty-one dollars a year at thirty dollars a bag rather than two hundred and six at twenty-two. That single change moves the cost per dozen and pushes break-even out by more than a year.

Your substitution price. A household that genuinely buys eight-dollar pastured eggs values the same production at a thousand dollars a year, and the flock breaks even in about thirteen months.

How many eggs you actually use. A hundred and twenty-five dozen is more than most households eat. If you use eighty dozen and give the rest away, your real saving is three hundred and twenty dollars, not five hundred, and break-even stretches accordingly. Selling the surplus, covered in Chapter 11, closes that gap.

Hens age. Book 3 notes that hens lay strongly for two to three years but live much longer. Sustained production means adding birds, which is a recurring cost the ten-year figure above should be understood to require.

Common Mistakes

Quoting the feed-only figure as though it were the true cost of an egg.

Quoting the year-one figure as though hens were a bad idea.

Forgetting that hens stop laying well after two or three years.

Counting all one hundred and twenty-five dozen as savings when the household eats eighty.

Buying an expensive prefabricated coop, which roughly doubles capital and break-even.

Comparing home eggs against premium retail to make the numbers look better than they are.

Budget Options

The free or near-free path: Build the coop and run from reclaimed lumber using Book 6 plans, keeping only hardware cloth and latches new. This can bring capital under four hundred dollars and break-even under two years, which is the single most effective change available.

The starter path: Build new to the Book 6 specification, buy feed in bulk at the best price you can store, and sell or trade surplus eggs to close the gap between production and household consumption.

Quick Wins

Build the coop rather than buying one; it is the largest single lever.

Find out your actual feed price per pound and use it.

Match flock size to what your household eats, or plan to sell the surplus.

Add pullets on a rotation so production does not fall off a cliff in year three.

Use the ten-year figure when deciding, not the year-one figure.

Chapter Checklist

[ ] I know my real capital cost, including the birds

[ ] I know my annual operating cost, especially feed

[ ] I know my realistic annual egg production

[ ] I have calculated cost per dozen on all three bases

[ ] I know my break-even point in years

[ ] I have matched flock size to consumption, or have a plan for surplus

[ ] I have budgeted for replacing hens as they age

Action Plan

Work the same five rows with your own numbers: your coop cost, your feed price, your flock size, your expected production, and the price you actually pay for eggs. Then compare your ten-year figure against that price. If it is lower, keeping hens saves you money on a decade view, and the next three years are an investment rather than a loss. The next chapter runs the same analysis for meat and milk.

Chapter 8: Meat and Milk - Worked Examples

What You'll Learn

This chapter runs the full calculation for two more enterprises: a rabbit breeding trio producing meat, and a pair of dairy goats producing milk. Both use the production figures established in Book 7, and both produce answers that are more favourable than eggs in one case and more demanding in the other.

Why It Matters

Meat and milk are the enterprises people assume are wildly uneconomic, and the arithmetic is more interesting than that. Rabbits break even faster than a flock of hens. Goats can break even quickly on paper and still be the wrong decision, for reasons the numbers alone do not show.

Rabbits: The Full Calculation

From Book 7, a breeding trio of one buck and two does, well managed at four litters per doe per year, produces about a hundred and nineteen pounds of dressed meat annually and consumes about one thousand and forty-two pounds of pellets.

What Home-Raised Rabbit Actually Costs

Line	Basis	Figure
Capital	Hutches, equipment, and breeding trio	488 dollars
Pellets	1042 pounds at 50 cents	521 dollars
Hay	annual	80 dollars
Bedding and consumables	annual	40 dollars
Total annual operating	every year	641 dollars
Annual production	dressed meat	119 pounds
Cost per pound, feed only	521 over 119	4 dollars 38 cents
Cost per pound, all operating	641 over 119	5 dollars 39 cents
Value at 7 dollars per pound	substitution rule	833 dollars
Annual surplus	833 less 641	192 dollars
Break-even	488 over 192	2.5 years

Rabbits break even faster than hens, at about two and a half years against three and a half, because the capital is much lower even though the annual feed bill is higher. That is a useful illustration of the principle from Chapter 6: capital, not operating cost, dominates break-even.

The honest note from Book 7 bears repeating here. At five dollars and thirty-nine cents a pound including all operating costs, home-raised rabbit is not cheap meat. It is roughly comparable to good butcher meat, produced in a space the size of a shed, with complete control over how the animals lived, plus a substantial supply of the best garden manure available.

Goats: The Full Calculation

From Book 7, two Nigerian Dwarf does each producing about a quart and a half a day across a roughly two hundred and eighty day lactation yield about a hundred and five gallons each, or two hundred and ten gallons a year between them.

What Home-Produced Goat Milk Costs

Line	Basis	Figure
Capital	Fencing, shelter, stand, and two does	1525 dollars
Hay	annual, two does	600 dollars
Grain	annual, while milking	300 dollars
Minerals and health	annual	50 dollars
Total annual operating	every year	950 dollars
Annual production	2 does at 105 gallons	210 gallons
Cost per gallon, all operating	950 over 210	4 dollars 52 cents
Value at 8 dollars per gallon	substitution rule	1680 dollars
Annual surplus	1680 less 950	730 dollars
Break-even	1525 over 730	2.1 years

On paper this is the best-performing enterprise in the book, breaking even in about two years and producing milk at four dollars and fifty-two cents a gallon against a retail substitution price of eight.

Now the part the arithmetic does not show, and this is the most important paragraph in the chapter.

That calculation assumes you actually use two hundred and ten gallons of milk a year, which is about four gallons a week, every week, for ten months. Most households do not. If you use half of it, the value halves to eight hundred and forty dollars, the annual result becomes a 110 dollar loss, and break-even disappears unless you use or sell more milk.

It also assumes you are milking twice a day, on schedule, for around ten months, and that you have somewhere for the kids to go each year. Book 7 covers both realities in detail. The financial case for goats is strong only for a household that genuinely consumes the milk or converts it reliably into cheese and yogurt. For anyone else, goats are a hobby enterprise, and Chapter 6's guidance applies: keep it if you want it, but name it honestly.

Comparing the Three

Meat, Milk, and Eggs Side by Side

Enterprise	Capital	Annual Surplus	Break-Even	Daily Time
Rabbit trio	488 dollars	192 dollars	2.5 years	5 to 10 minutes
Two dairy goats	1525 dollars	730 dollars	2.1 years	45 to 90 minutes
Six hens	823 dollars	239 dollars	3.4 years	10 minutes

Read the last column alongside the fourth. Goats show the shortest break-even and consume roughly six times the daily time of the other two combined. If you value your hours at all, as Chapter 1 discussed, that changes the ranking completely, which is exactly why this book tracks time in hours rather than burying it in the money.

Common Mistakes

Assuming home-raised meat is cheap; it is comparable to good butcher meat, not to supermarket chicken.

Running the goat calculation without checking whether your household actually drinks two hundred gallons of milk.

Ignoring the daily time cost, which is where goats differ most from every other enterprise.

Forgetting that goats produce kids annually that must be sold, kept, or eaten.

Comparing rabbit against premium retail rabbit rather than against the meat you actually buy.

Overlooking that rabbit manure has real garden value not counted in these figures.

Budget Options

The free or near-free path: Build hutches and goat shelter from Book 6 plans, buy a doe already in milk rather than raising kids for a year, and use cattle panels for fencing. Cutting capital is the fastest route to break-even in both enterprises.

The starter path: Quality breeding stock, proper fencing, and bulk feed give predictable production and the figures above, with rabbits the better first choice by a wide margin for anyone new to livestock.

Quick Wins

Choose rabbits before goats if you want meat with a short payback and little daily time.

Check your household's real milk consumption before buying goats.

Count the manure as a genuine return on the rabbitry.

Buy hay in bulk at the right season, since it is the largest goat cost.

Track your hours as well as your dollars.

Chapter Checklist

[ ] I have calculated capital, operating, production, and break-even for my enterprise

[ ] I have used my own substitution prices, not the examples

[ ] I have checked that my household actually consumes what the enterprise produces

[ ] I have accounted for the daily time cost, not just the money

[ ] I have a plan for goat kids if I keep goats

[ ] I know whether this is an investment or a hobby, and I am at peace with the answer

Action Plan

Run the full calculation for whichever enterprise you are considering, using your own figures. Then apply the consumption test: multiply your realistic annual production by the share your household will actually use, and recalculate. If the enterprise still shows a surplus, it is an investment. If it does not, it is a hobby, and you should decide about it on that basis. The next chapter applies the same treatment to the garden.

Chapter 9: The Garden - A Full Worked Example

What You'll Learn

This chapter runs the same calculation for a single raised bed, and then addresses the question that matters more in a garden than in any animal enterprise: which crops are actually worth growing if saving money is your aim.

Why It Matters

The garden is where most homesteads begin and where the economics are best, because capital is low and the payback is fast. It is also where crop choice makes an enormous difference. Two gardeners with identical beds and identical effort can differ by a factor of five in what their harvest is worth, purely through what they chose to plant.

The Setup

One four-by-eight raised bed built to the Book 6 specification, which gives an inside growing area of ninety-three by forty-five inches, or just over twenty-nine square feet of actual planting space. Note that this is less than the thirty-two square feet the outside dimensions suggest, because the bed's own boards take up room, which is the sort of detail that matters when you are planning spacing from Book 2.

One Raised Bed, Fully Costed

Line	Basis	Figure
Capital	Bed, soil, and fasteners from Book 6	191 dollars
Usable growing area	93 by 45 inches	29 square feet
Annual operating	Seeds, transplants, amendments	50 dollars
Annual production	mixed vegetables	60 pounds
Value at 3 dollars per pound	substitution rule	180 dollars
Annual surplus	180 less 50	130 dollars
Break-even	191 over 130	1.5 years
Cost per pound, year one	241 over 60	4 dollars 2 cents
Cost per pound, steady state	50 over 60	83 cents
Cost per pound, ten-year average	691 over 600	1 dollar 15 cents

A raised bed pays for itself in about a season and a half, faster than any other project in this series, and after that it produces vegetables at eighty-three cents a pound against a substitution price of three dollars. This is why every book in this series recommends starting with the garden.

Grow What Is Expensive to Buy

Here is the insight that changes garden economics more than any other, and it is routinely ignored.

The value of your harvest depends far less on how much you grow than on what you grow. A square foot of salad greens, harvested repeatedly across a season, can return many times what a square foot of potatoes returns, because greens are expensive to buy and potatoes are not.

Consider what you actually pay. Fresh herbs cost an absurd amount per pound in a supermarket and grow like weeds. Salad leaves are expensive, perishable, and can be cut repeatedly. Cherry tomatoes, sugar snap peas, and green beans all command high prices and produce heavily in small spaces. Meanwhile potatoes, onions, carrots, and cabbage are among the cheapest food in any shop, take a full season, and occupy space the entire time.

None of this means you should not grow potatoes. It means that if your goal is saving money, potatoes are the wrong crop, and a bed of herbs and salad greens will out-earn a bed of roots several times over.

What to Grow If You Are Growing to Save Money

Crop Group	Return per Square Foot	Why
Fresh herbs	Highest	Very expensive to buy, tiny space, cut repeatedly
Salad and cutting greens	Very high	Expensive, perishable, multiple harvests
Cherry and slicing tomatoes	High	High price, heavy yield, long season
Beans and peas	High	Good price, vertical growing, productive
Summer squash and cucumbers	Moderate	Productive but cheap to buy in season
Root vegetables and brassicas	Low	Cheap to buy, occupy space all season
Potatoes, onions, and grains	Lowest	Among the cheapest food available

The Other Multipliers

Three further factors move garden returns substantially.

Succession planting. A bed that grows one crop and then sits empty produces once. A bed that follows spring greens with summer beans and then autumn greens produces three times from the same capital. The cold frame from Book 6 extends this at both ends of the year.

Vertical growing. The trellis from Book 6 lets beans, peas, and cucumbers occupy vertical space, which raises production per square foot without any additional bed.

Your own compost. The compost system from Book 5 replaces bought amendments, which is a significant share of the fifty-dollar annual operating cost, and it converts waste you already have into an input you would otherwise buy.

Together these can plausibly double the annual value of a single bed without any additional capital, which halves the break-even period.

Common Mistakes

Growing mainly the cheapest crops in the shop and wondering why the savings are small.

Leaving beds empty for months rather than succession planting.

Buying transplants for everything when seed is a fraction of the cost.

Buying soil amendments while compostable material goes in the bin.

Building new beds every year, so earlier capital never pays off.

Growing more of a crop than the household will eat or preserve.

Budget Options

The free or near-free path: Build the bed from reclaimed lumber, fill partly with the hugelkultur method described in Book 6 to reduce purchased soil, start everything from seed, save seed from open-pollinated crops, and use compost from Book 5 in place of bought amendments. This can reduce both capital and operating cost dramatically.

The starter path: One well-built cedar bed, good soil, quality seed, and a compost system, planted in succession with high-value crops, is the fastest-paying project in this entire series.

Quick Wins

Plant herbs and salad greens before anything else; they return the most per square foot.

Succession plant so no bed sits empty in the growing season.

Start from seed rather than buying transplants.

Grow vertically using the trellis from Book 6.

Use your own compost instead of buying amendments.

Skip potatoes and onions if your goal is saving money.

Chapter Checklist

[ ] I know my bed's actual usable growing area

[ ] I have calculated capital, operating, production, and break-even

[ ] I am prioritising high-value crops over cheap staples

[ ] I am succession planting rather than leaving beds empty

[ ] I am growing vertically where I can

[ ] I am using my own compost rather than buying amendments

[ ] I am growing what my household will actually eat or preserve

Action Plan

Work out your own bed's usable area and its real cost, then plan next season's planting around value rather than habit. Put herbs and cutting greens in the most accessible spots, plan two or three successions across the season, and set up the compost system from Book 5 if you have not already. Then compare your steady-state cost per pound against what you pay in the shop. The next chapter answers the question that most affects every capital figure in this book.

Chapter 10: Build or Buy

What You'll Learn

This chapter answers the question that moves homestead capital more than any other: whether to build your infrastructure or buy it. You will see a direct comparison using the projects from Book 6, and a framework for deciding when building is genuinely worth it and when it is not.

Why It Matters

Chapter 6 established that capital, not operating cost, dominates break-even. This chapter is therefore the single largest financial lever available to a homesteader, and the difference is not marginal. Across the main projects in this series, building rather than buying saves roughly half.

The Direct Comparison

Every build cost below is the verified figure from Book 6. The purchase prices are typical for comparable ready-made items.

What Building It Yourself Saves

Project	Build Cost	Typical Purchase Price	Saving
Raised bed, 4 by 8	191 dollars	320 dollars	129 dollars
Cold frame	96 dollars	220 dollars	124 dollars
Three-bin compost system	194 dollars	400 dollars	206 dollars
Chicken coop for six hens	457 dollars	900 dollars	443 dollars
Potting bench	53 dollars	180 dollars	127 dollars
All five projects	991 dollars	2020 dollars	1029 dollars

Building these five projects saves about a thousand dollars, or slightly over half the purchase price. Applied to the egg enterprise in Chapter 7, halving the coop cost reduces break-even from about three and a half years to under two.

Quality, Not Just Cost

The saving is only half the argument. The other half is that a bought coop of the same nominal capacity is frequently worse.

Book 3 makes the point directly: commercial coops are routinely advertised for more birds than they can house at four square feet each, and many use materials and latches that a determined raccoon defeats. A coop you build to the Book 6 specification is sized correctly, uses half-inch hardware cloth, and has latches you chose.

So building is usually cheaper and better, which is an unusual combination.

When Buying Is the Right Call

Buying makes sense in several genuine situations, and it is not a failure to choose it.

When time is the binding constraint rather than money. A coop is a multi-weekend project, as Book 6 states plainly, and if the chicks are already six weeks old and outgrowing the brooder, buying is the correct decision.

When you lack the tools and would need to buy them for a single project. Chapter 1 of Book 6 keeps the tool list short, but a saw and drill you will never use again are part of the true cost.

When the item is precision-made or safety-critical in a way a home build is not, which for this series means things like a pressure canner, an incubator, or a heated waterer, none of which should be improvised.

When physical ability makes the build impractical. This is a legitimate constraint and not worth arguing with.

The Middle Path

Two hybrids are worth knowing.

Buy the materials and have someone else build to the plan. This retains the specification and the quality while removing the labour, and typically still costs well under a finished commercial product.

Build the simple things and buy the complex ones. Raised beds, compost bins, benches, and trellises are genuinely easy, and their savings are proportionally large. If the coop is the one project you buy, you still capture most of the benefit across everything else.

Reclaimed Material

Building from reclaimed lumber, salvaged windows, and pallet wood reduces capital further, sometimes to almost nothing, and Book 6 gives a free or near-free path for every project.

The one rule, stated in Books 3, 6, and 7 alike: buy the hardware cloth and the predator-proof latches new. Those are what stand between your animals and everything that wants to eat them, and they are a small share of the total cost. Economise everywhere else.

Common Mistakes

Buying infrastructure without pricing the build, and doubling your capital unnecessarily.

Buying a commercial coop rated for more birds than it can actually house.

Building when time, not money, was the real constraint, and missing the deadline.

Buying tools for a single project without counting them in the comparison.

Improvising equipment that should be bought properly, such as a pressure canner.

Using reclaimed hardware cloth or old latches to save a few dollars.

Budget Options

The free or near-free path: Build everything from reclaimed material with Book 6 plans, buying only hardware cloth, latches, and fasteners. This is the largest single reduction in capital available anywhere in this series and it roughly halves every break-even period in this book.

The starter path: Build the simple projects yourself and buy or commission only the most complex, capturing most of the saving without the whole time commitment.

Quick Wins

Price the build before you buy anything.

Build the simple projects first; their savings are proportionally largest.

Count any tools you must buy in the comparison.

Buy hardware cloth and latches new, always.

Consider buying materials and hiring the labour as a middle path.

Chapter Checklist

[ ] I have priced building against buying for each project

[ ] I have counted any tools I would need to buy

[ ] I have honestly assessed whether time or money is my constraint

[ ] I am building the simple projects at minimum

[ ] I am buying new hardware cloth and latches regardless

[ ] I am buying rather than improvising anything safety-critical

Action Plan

Before your next infrastructure purchase, price the same item as a build using Book 6, including any tools you lack. If the saving is meaningful and you have the weekend, build it, and note how much that single decision moves the break-even figure you calculated in Chapter 6. The next chapter covers the two remaining levers: reducing what you spend and earning from what you produce.

Chapter 11: Cutting Costs and Selling Surplus

What You'll Learn

This chapter covers the two remaining levers: reducing what a homestead costs to run, and earning something from what it produces beyond your own needs. It also covers, in general terms, the legal reality of selling food, which is more restrictive than most beginners assume.

Why It Matters

Chapter 4 established that feed is seventy to eighty percent of operating cost in any animal enterprise. Chapter 5 established that production beyond what your household consumes is worth far less than grocery value unless you sell it. Those two facts define exactly where the remaining money is.

Reducing Feed Cost

Buy in bulk, within the limit of your storage. The per-pound price falls meaningfully with bag size and falls further if you can take delivery by the pallet. The constraint is dry, rodent-proof storage and using it before it goes stale, which for most feeds means a few months.

Buy with other keepers. A group of local homesteaders ordering together can often access pricing that none of them could alone. This is the most underused cost reduction in small livestock.

Time your hay purchase. Hay bought straight from the field at first cutting costs substantially less than hay bought from a store in February. For goat keepers this is the largest single saving available, since hay is the dominant cost.

Use forage and surplus sensibly. Garden surplus, weeds, and trimmings genuinely reduce feed bills for poultry and rabbits, though not dramatically. Geese are the exception, grazing most of their summer diet, as Book 7 explains. Treat forage as a useful supplement rather than a replacement, and introduce any change gradually, particularly with rabbits.

Reduce waste. Feeders that spill, rodents in the feed store, and hay trodden into mud can waste a surprising share of what you buy. Proper feeders and storage pay for themselves quickly.

Reducing Other Costs

Compost from Book 5 replaces bought soil amendments entirely, converting waste into an input. Seed saved from open-pollinated crops removes most of a garden's annual seed cost. Starting from seed rather than buying transplants cuts the same line further. Deep-litter bedding, topped up rather than replaced, stretches bedding and produces compost. Hatching your own replacements rather than buying chicks or kits removes the replacement-stock line, though it requires an incubator for quail, as Book 7 notes.

Cost Reductions Ranked by Impact

Action	Applies To	Typical Impact
Build rather than buy infrastructure	All enterprises	Largest; roughly halves capital
Buy feed in bulk or as a group	All animals	Large; feed is most of operating cost
Buy hay at first cutting	Goats and rabbits	Large for goats specifically
Use own compost	Garden	Removes most amendment cost
Save seed and start from seed	Garden	Removes most seed cost
Hatch or breed replacements	Poultry, quail, rabbits	Removes replacement stock line
Reduce feed waste	All animals	Moderate and immediate

Selling Surplus: The Legal Reality First

Before the opportunities, the constraint, because this is where enthusiasm meets regulation and the rules are stricter than most people expect.

Selling eggs in small quantities directly to consumers is permitted in many places with light or no licensing, but requirements vary considerably by jurisdiction and commonly cover labelling, refrigeration, candling, and where you may sell. Some allow farm-gate sales only and prohibit farmers markets without a licence.

Selling meat is heavily regulated essentially everywhere. In most jurisdictions, meat sold to others must be processed in an inspected facility, which means home-processed rabbit or poultry generally cannot be sold legally, whatever the local custom.

Selling raw milk is among the most tightly regulated activities in food law, prohibited outright in many places and restricted in most others. Cheese and other dairy products made at home for sale face similar constraints.

Cottage food laws in many jurisdictions permit sale of certain low-risk prepared foods made in a home kitchen, typically baked goods, jams, and dried products, and typically exclude anything requiring refrigeration, which excludes most dairy and all meat.

The practical guidance is simple: producing for your own household is essentially unregulated, and selling is not. Check your specific local and state rules before advertising anything, and treat the sale of meat and dairy as prohibited unless you have confirmed otherwise. Nothing in this book is legal advice.

What Actually Sells Well

Within those limits, several things reliably sell at a small scale.

Surplus eggs are the classic, and at farm-gate prices they close the gap between production and household consumption that Chapter 7 identified.

Started seedlings in spring are unusually profitable relative to effort, since seed costs pennies and a healthy transplant sells for a few dollars. A cold frame from Book 6 makes this straightforward.

Breeding stock and started animals sell steadily. Rabbit kits, started quail, and goat kids all have local markets, and selling stock is generally far less regulated than selling meat, since you are selling a live animal rather than food.

Compost, worm castings, and rabbit manure sell to gardeners. Rabbit manure in particular is prized precisely because it can be used immediately, as Book 7 explains.

Value-added goods such as soap, dried herbs, and jams may be permitted under cottage food rules where you live.

Bartering

Trading is common in homesteading circles, straightforward, and typically outside the regulatory issues that attach to sales, though it may still have tax implications in some jurisdictions. Eggs for hay, seedlings for labour, rabbit manure for firewood. It converts genuine surplus into something you would otherwise buy, which is economically identical to a sale and often easier.

Keep It Honest in the Accounts

Income from surplus belongs in the records from Chapter 2 as money in, against the enterprise that produced it. It is genuinely the fastest route to break-even for any over-producing enterprise: the flock from Chapter 7 that produces a hundred and twenty-five dozen against a household that eats eighty reaches break-even considerably sooner if the remaining forty-five dozen are sold rather than given away.

Common Mistakes

Advertising eggs, meat, or milk without checking local rules first.

Assuming home-processed meat can be sold because neighbours do it.

Buying feed in small bags because storage was never sorted out.

Buying hay in winter at the worst price of the year.

Letting surplus rot rather than selling, trading, or preserving it.

Expecting surplus sales to be a meaningful income rather than a useful offset.

Budget Options

The free or near-free path: Bulk feed buying, own compost, saved seed, and bartering surplus require no investment at all and address the largest cost lines directly.

The starter path: Proper feed storage, a cold frame for spring seedlings, and a small regular egg customer base turn a break-even homestead into one that funds its own expansion.

Quick Wins

Sort out dry, rodent-proof storage so you can buy feed in bulk.

Find other local keepers and order feed together.

Buy hay at first cutting, not in February.

Check your local rules before selling anything, and treat meat and dairy as off limits until confirmed.

Sell or trade genuine surplus rather than letting it go to waste.

Sell spring seedlings; the margin relative to effort is excellent.

Chapter Checklist

[ ] I buy feed in the largest quantity I can store properly

[ ] I have explored group buying with other local keepers

[ ] I buy hay at the right season

[ ] I use my own compost instead of buying amendments

[ ] I have checked the actual rules for selling eggs where I live

[ ] I understand that selling meat and raw dairy is generally prohibited

[ ] Surplus is sold, traded, or preserved rather than wasted

[ ] Money in is recorded against the enterprise that produced it

Action Plan

Start with storage, because it unlocks bulk buying, which is the largest operating saving available. Then find one other local keeper to buy feed with. Look up your jurisdiction's rules on egg sales specifically, and write down what they require. Finally, identify your single largest genuine surplus and decide whether to sell it, trade it, or preserve it. The last chapter puts all of this into a five-year plan.

Chapter 12: Your Five-Year Homestead Budget

What You'll Learn

This final chapter assembles everything into a five-year plan. You will see a year-by-year build sequence with cumulative cash position, understand why the third year is the hardest and the fourth is when it turns, and learn to reinvest surplus so the homestead funds its own growth.

Why It Matters

Every calculation in this book has been about a single enterprise. A homestead is several, built in sequence, and the interesting question is what the whole thing looks like over the years it takes to mature. The answer explains both why so many people quit in year two and why those who do not are glad they stayed.

The Five-Year Model

This plan builds one raised bed in year one, a coop and flock in year two, and a rabbit trio in year three, then simply runs everything from year four onward. All figures come from the chapters above.

What the First Five Years Actually Look Like

Year	Capital Added	Annual Surplus Produced	Net for the Year	Cumulative Position
Year 1	191 dollars, raised bed	130 dollars	minus 61 dollars	minus 61 dollars
Year 2	823 dollars, coop and flock	369 dollars	minus 454 dollars	minus 515 dollars
Year 3	488 dollars, rabbit trio	561 dollars	plus 73 dollars	minus 442 dollars
Year 4	none	561 dollars	plus 561 dollars	plus 119 dollars
Year 5	none	561 dollars	plus 561 dollars	plus 680 dollars

Read that cumulative column carefully, because it is the most honest picture of homestead economics in this series.

Year two is the worst. You have added the largest capital item, the coop, and its production has barely begun. The cumulative position is more than five hundred dollars underwater. This is precisely when most people conclude it is not working.

Year three roughly holds. The enterprises are producing enough to cover the new capital, but the earlier deficit is still there.

Year four is when it turns. With no new capital, the full surplus flows through and the cumulative position goes positive. From here every year adds roughly five hundred and sixty dollars.

Why Year Two Feels Like Failure

It is worth naming what year two does to a beginner, because forewarning genuinely helps.

In year two you are spending the most and receiving the least. The coop is built but the pullets are not yet laying well. Feed bills have started and egg production has not caught up. You are five hundred dollars down, you have been working every weekend, and the grocery bill has barely moved.

Nothing is wrong. That is what year two looks like on a correctly executed plan. The model above is built from verified figures throughout this series, and it goes underwater in year two by design, because that is what capital investment does.

The people who quit in year two are not making a mistake about the arithmetic. They simply do not know that year four exists.

Making It Turn Faster

Three changes materially shorten the underwater period.

Build from reclaimed material. Chapter 10 showed that building rather than buying roughly halves capital. Applied to this plan, it removes several hundred dollars from years one through three and pulls break-even forward by roughly a year.

Sell the genuine surplus. Chapter 11 showed that the flock produces well beyond most households' consumption. Selling forty-five dozen eggs a year at farm-gate prices adds meaningfully to the annual surplus and compounds every year thereafter.

Sequence by payback, not by enthusiasm. The plan above deliberately builds the fastest-paying project first. Building the coop in year one instead would deepen the trough and delay the turn.

Reinvesting

Once the cumulative position turns positive, the most powerful thing you can do is reinvest the surplus into the next enterprise rather than absorbing it into general spending.

Year five's five hundred and sixty dollars funds a second raised bed and a cold frame with money to spare, and those pay back in a season and a half. The homestead then funds its own expansion permanently, which is the point at which it stops being a cost and becomes a system.

This is why the last chapter of Book 6 recommends building projects in sequence, and why Book 7 recommends adding one species at a time. Both are the operational form of the same financial principle.

A Seasonal Budget

Because homestead spending is seasonal, as Chapter 1 established, an annual figure is not enough to plan with.

A Seasonal Spending Pattern

Season	Main Spending	Main Returns
Late winter	Seeds, chicks, build materials	Very little
Spring	Transplants, soil, stock, feed	First greens and eggs
Summer	Feed, hay at first cutting	Peak garden production
Autumn	Feed, bedding, winter preparation	Harvest, preserving, processing
Winter	Feed, replacement planning	Reduced eggs, stored food

Set money aside in autumn for the late winter and spring peak. That single habit prevents most homestead cash-flow trouble, and it is the practical reason the seasonal review in Chapter 2 matters.

Common Mistakes

Quitting in year two, without knowing that year four exists.

Building the most expensive project first, deepening and lengthening the trough.

Buying infrastructure rather than building it, which roughly doubles the time underwater.

Absorbing the surplus into general spending instead of reinvesting it.

Budgeting monthly for spending that is overwhelmingly seasonal.

Adding a new enterprise every year, so the plan never reaches the years where earlier capital pays.

Budget Options

The free or near-free path: Build everything from reclaimed material, start with the raised bed, sell or trade all genuine surplus, and reinvest every dollar of it. This version of the plan goes positive substantially earlier than the model above.

The starter path: Follow the sequence as written, building to the Book 6 specifications with new materials, and accept that year two is underwater by design. The infrastructure lasts a decade and the returns from year four are durable.

Quick Wins

Build the fastest-paying project first, which is the raised bed.

Expect year two to be the hardest, and plan for it rather than being surprised.

Set money aside in autumn for the spring spending peak.

Reinvest surplus into the next enterprise rather than absorbing it.

Stop adding capital for a year and let the existing projects pay off.

Chapter Checklist

[ ] I have a multi-year plan rather than a single-season one

[ ] I am building in order of payback, cheapest and fastest first

[ ] I know which year will be the hardest, and why

[ ] I have a seasonal setting-aside habit for spring spending

[ ] I have a plan to sell or trade genuine surplus

[ ] I intend to reinvest surplus into the next enterprise

[ ] I have scheduled at least one year with no new capital

Action Plan

Write out your own five-year plan on one page: what you will build each year, its capital cost, and the annual surplus it should produce once running. Order it so the fastest-paying projects come first. Mark the year you expect to be deepest underwater and make peace with it now. Then set aside money each autumn for the spring ahead, and when the cumulative position turns positive, put it straight back into the next project. That is the whole of homestead budgeting, and it is the last thing this series has to teach you.

Conclusion

This is the last chapter of the last book in The Homestead Starter Series, and it is worth saying plainly what the numbers in this book add up to.

Homesteading does not save money quickly. A raised bed pays for itself in about a season and a half, which is fast. A flock of hens takes three and a half years. A whole small homestead of garden, flock, and rabbits spends most of three years underwater before the cumulative position turns positive in year four. Anyone who told you otherwise was selling something.

What homesteading does is convert a one-time investment into a durable annual return. From year four, that example homestead produces around fifteen hundred dollars of food a year against roughly nine hundred and fifty dollars of running costs, on infrastructure already paid for, and it goes on doing that for as long as the coop stands and the beds hold soil. That is not a get-rich scheme. It is a slow, reliable, compounding improvement in your household's position, and it is real.

The rest of what you get does not appear in any table in this book. Eggs from hens you know. Vegetables picked an hour before dinner. Meat from animals you raised the way you chose. Skills that do not expire, and a household that is a little less dependent on things outside its control. This book has deliberately kept those out of the arithmetic, not because they do not matter but because they matter too much to be used as an excuse for bad numbers.

Across eight books this series has tried to do one thing consistently: tell you the truth, including the parts that are inconvenient. That a coop must be built before the chicks outgrow the brooder. That rabbits handle cold well and heat badly. That goats will test every fence you build. That a 2x4 is not two inches by four. That home-raised rabbit costs about five dollars and thirty-nine cents a pound, which is not cheap. Every figure in these books was worked out rather than asserted, because a beginner deserves numbers that hold up.

You now have everything the series can give you: how to choose and plan a homestead, how to grow in raised beds, how to keep hens, how to preserve what you produce, how to build soil, how to build the structures, how to keep small livestock, and how to know what all of it costs and when it pays.

Start with the raised bed. Build it this weekend. Expect year two to be hard. Keep going, because year four is real and it is closer than it looks from here.

About the Author

Hudson Briggs is a lifelong DIY enthusiast, gardener, and homesteading educator dedicated to helping everyday people become more self-sufficient. Through practical guidance, realistic budgets, and beginner-friendly instruction, he helps readers build skills that lead to greater independence, confidence, and resilience.

The Homestead Starter Series

Book 1 - The Beginner's Guide to Homesteading Book 2 - Raised Bed Gardening Book 3 - Backyard Chickens Book 4 - Food Preservation Book 5 - Composting Made Simple Book 6 - Homestead Projects Book 7 - Small Livestock for Beginners Book 8 - Homestead Budgeting

Disclaimer: The information in this book is provided for general educational purposes and is not financial, tax, legal, or accounting advice. All prices, costs, yields, and returns are illustrative examples based on the figures used elsewhere in this series; actual results vary considerably by region, season, scale, market conditions, and individual circumstance, and no particular financial outcome is promised or implied. Regulations governing the sale of eggs, meat, dairy, and prepared foods vary by jurisdiction and change over time, so confirm the rules applicable to you before selling anything, and consult qualified professionals regarding tax and legal obligations. The author and publisher assume no responsibility for outcomes resulting from the use of this information.

www.ingramcontent.com/pod-product-compliance
Lightning Source LLC
LaVergne TN
LVHW100733061126
851857LV00011B/524
* 9 7 9 8 2 4 0 8 2 6 2 8 3 *